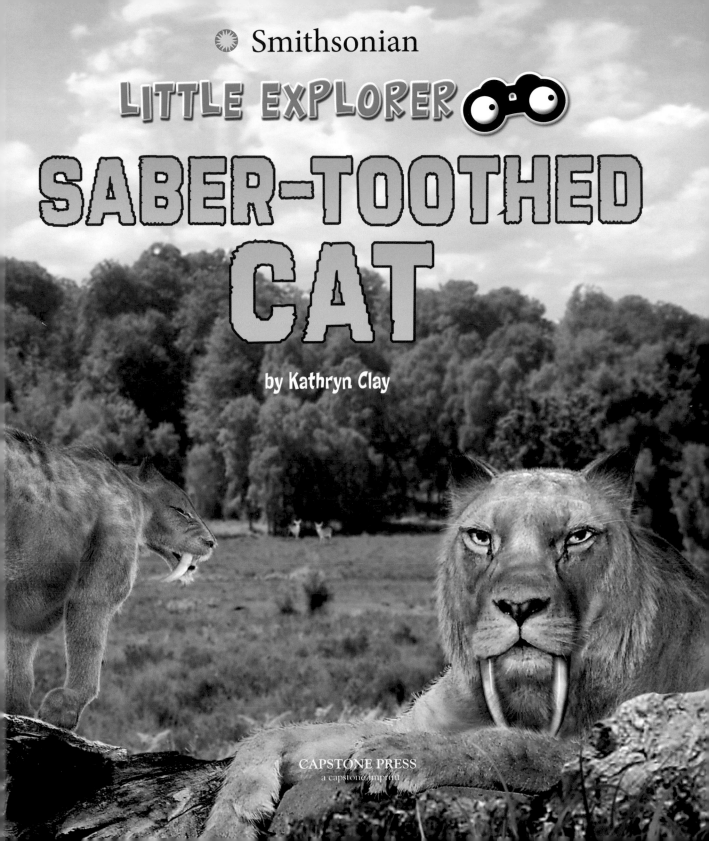

Smithsonian

LITTLE EXPLORER

SABER-TOOTHED CAT

by Kathryn Clay

CAPSTONE PRESS
a capstone imprint

Little Explorer is published by Capstone Press,
1710 Roe Crest Drive, North Mankato, Minnesota 56003
www.mycapstone.com

The name of the Smithsonian Institution and the sunburst
logo are registered trademarks of the Smithsonian Institution.
For more information, please visit www.si.edu.

Library of Congress Cataloging-in-Publication Data
Names: Clay, Kathryn, author.
Title: Saber-toothed cat / by Kathryn Clay.
Description: North Mankato, Minnesota : Capstone Press, 2018.
| Series: Smithsonian little explorer. Little paleontologist |
Audience: Age 5–9.
Identifiers: LCCN 2017046962| ISBN 9781543505382 (library
binding) | ISBN 9781543505443 (paperback)
Subjects: LCSH: Saber-toothed tigers—Juvenile literature.
Classification: LCC QE882.C15 C53 2018 | DDC 569/.75—dc23
LC record available at https://lccn.loc.gov/2017046962

Editorial Credits
Michelle Hasselius, editor; Heidi Thompson, designer;
Eric Gohl, media researcher; Kathy McColley, production specialist

Our very special thanks to Matthew T. Miller, Paleontologist in
the Department of Paleobiology at the National Museum of
Natural History, Smithsonian Institution, for his review. Capstone
would also like to thank Kealy Gordon, Product Development
Manager, and the following at Smithsonian Enterprises: Ellen
Nanney, Licensing Manager; Brigid Ferraro, Vice President,
Education and Consumer Products; Carol LeBlanc, Senior Vice
President, Education and Consumer Products; and Christopher A.
Liedel, President.

Image Credits
Alamy: Stocktrek Images, Inc., 11, 24 (bottom); Capstone: Jon Hughes,
cover, 1, 2–3, 4–5, 8–9, 12, 13, 18–19, 20–21, 28–29, 30–31; Newscom:
Universal Images Group/De Agostini Picture Library, 16, Universal
Images Group/Dorling Kindersley, 6–7; Science Source: Spencer
Sutton, 25; Shutterstock: Akkharat Jarusilawong, 14–15, 27, Chtistophe
Rolland, 14 (inset), Esteban De Armas, 17 (bottom), Julie Clopper,
24 (top), New SIGHT Photography, 17 (top), Stocksnapper, 5 (inset),
W. Scott McGill, 26

Printed and bound in Canada.
010814S8

TABLE OF CONTENTS

name: saber-toothed cat

how to say it: SAY-bur-toothed CAT

when it lived: Pleistocene Epoch, Cenozoic Era

what it ate: meat

size: 7 feet (2.1 meters) long
4 feet (1.2 m) tall at
the shoulders
weighed up to 800 pounds
(363 kilograms)

The saber-toothed cat was a large meat-eating animal. Along with woolly mammoths and mastodons, it lived during the last Ice Age. Now all three of these animals are extinct.

Thanks to FOSSILS

A fossil is evidence of life from the geologic past. Fossil bones, teeth, and tracks found in the earth have taught us everything we know about saber-toothed cats.

the skull of a saber-toothed cat

LONG AND STRONG

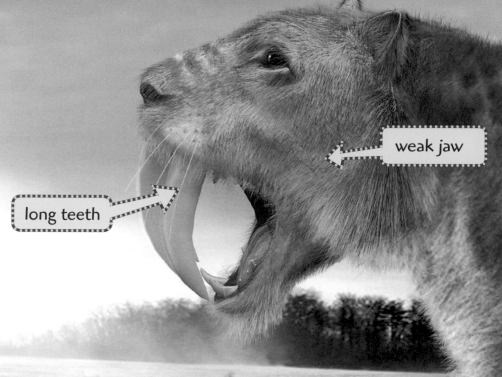

long teeth

long teeth

weak jaw

sharp claws

Saber-toothed cats looked similar to African lions without their manes. Saber-toothed cats were smaller than today's lions but weighed almost twice as much because of their strong bodies.

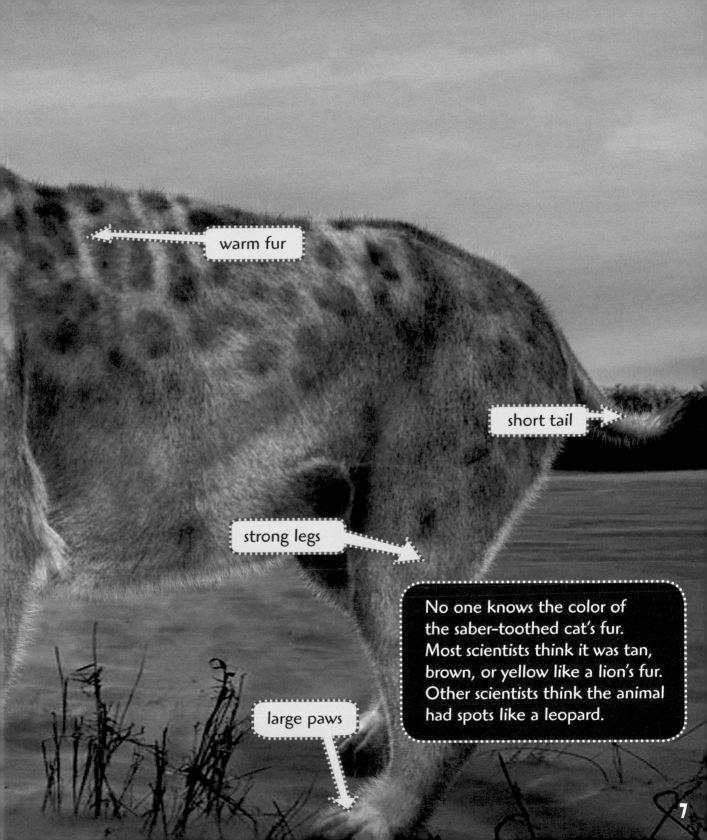

warm fur

short tail

strong legs

large paws

No one knows the color of the saber-toothed cat's fur. Most scientists think it was tan, brown, or yellow like a lion's fur. Other scientists think the animal had spots like a leopard.

A CAT WITH MANY NAMES

Saber-toothed cats are also known as saber-toothed tigers. But these cats were not related to tigers.

Smilodon means "knife tooth."

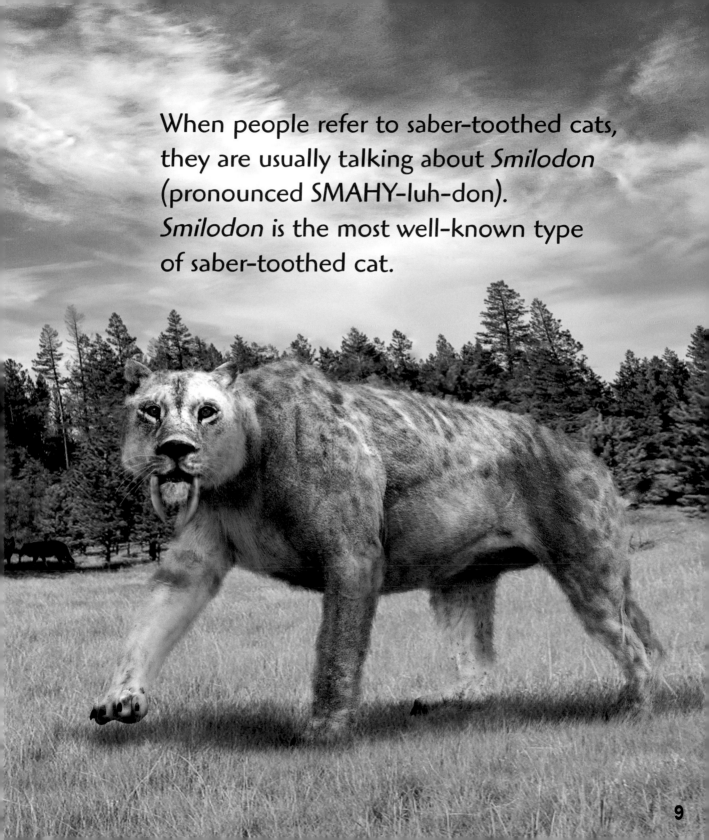

When people refer to saber-toothed cats, they are usually talking about *Smilodon* (pronounced SMAHY-luh-don). *Smilodon* is the most well-known type of saber-toothed cat.

OTHER SABERS

There were two other kinds of saber-toothed cats. Both were related to *Smilodon*.

Megantereon lived before *Smilodon*, about 10 million to 500,000 years ago. It made its home in North America, Europe, Asia, and Africa. At about 100 pounds (45 kg), *Megantereon* was about the size of a Great Dane.

The largest saber-toothed cat was *Machairodus*. *Machairodus* also lived before *Smilodon* throughout North America, Europe, Africa, and Asia. *Machairodus* weighed nearly 900 pounds (408 kg), about the size of a polar bear.

Machairodus means "dagger tooth."

TERRIFYING TEETH

Smilodon is known for its two large canine teeth. The teeth grew nearly 8 inches (20 centimeters) long and could easily stab prey. Just one bite could kill a small animal.

Smilodon's teeth were so large that they stuck out of its mouth. To protect its teeth, the cat had to be careful when eating prey. Biting down too hard might break a tooth.

Some scientists think *Smilodon's* large teeth may have been used to attract a mate.

A MIGHTY MOUTH

Scientists examined the bones in *Smilodon's* throat to find out what sounds the animal made. The bones looked like a lion's throat bones. This means *Smilodon* probably roared like a lion.

"Smilodon was an awesome beast, and what it lacked in bite force it more than made up for elsewhere."
—paleontologist Stephen Wroe

Smilodon opened its mouth wide to eat. Modern cats cannot open their mouths as wide.

Despite its large mouth, *Smilodon* did not have a strong bite. Its jaws could only apply 200 pounds (91 kg) of pressure. A modern lion's jaws can apply 660 pounds (299 kg) of pressure.

SHORT BUT STRONG

Smilodon had short legs, which meant the animal couldn't chase after quick prey. But *Smilodon's* legs were thick and strong. Its powerful front legs could hold and wrestle prey to the ground.

Smilodon fossil footprints suggest its paws were 7.6 inches (19.3 cm) across. That's larger than a Bengal tiger's paws.

Saber-toothed cats ate woolly mammoths, mastodons, ancient horses, bison, and early humans.

PATIENT PREDATOR

The saber-toothed cat hid behind bushes when hunting. When prey came close, *Smilodon* would pounce on the unsuspecting animal. After wrestling its prey, *Smilodon* stabbed its teeth into the soft flesh.

Smilodon could retract its fierce claws, like a cat can today. Its claws only came out when they were being used.

BETTER TOGETHER

Scientists think saber-toothed cats hunted and traveled in packs, like many big cats do today. Hunting together allowed the group to attack larger animals.

Scientists have discovered *Smilodon* fossils with broken bones that show signs of healing. Cats with serious injuries would not be able to catch prey and feed themselves. They most likely survived because other *Smilodons* shared their food.

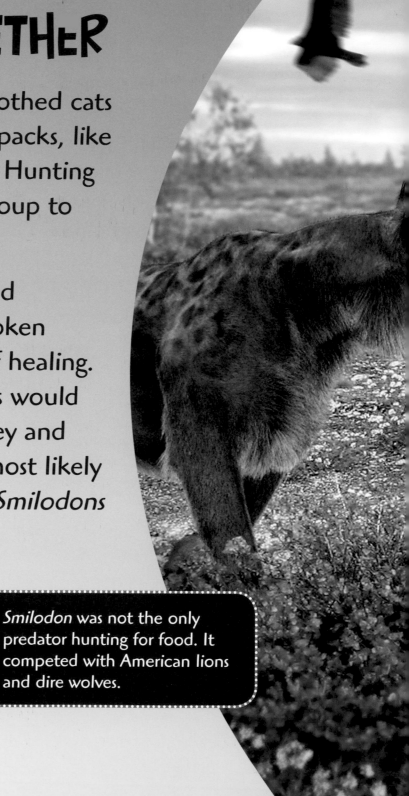

Smilodon was not the only predator hunting for food. It competed with American lions and dire wolves.

PLEISTOCENE HOME

Aside from birds, dinosaurs became extinct long before *Smilodon* existed. *Smilodon* lived at the same time as early humans.

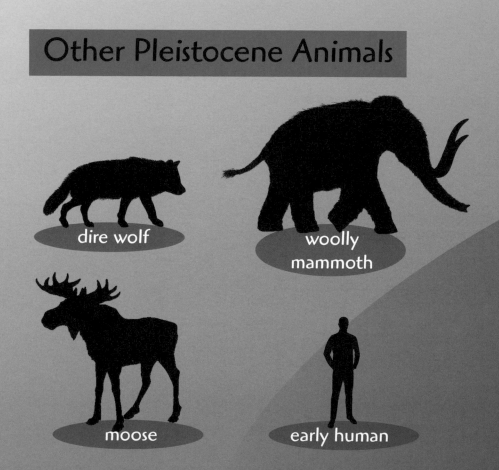

Other Pleistocene Animals

dire wolf

woolly mammoth

moose

early human

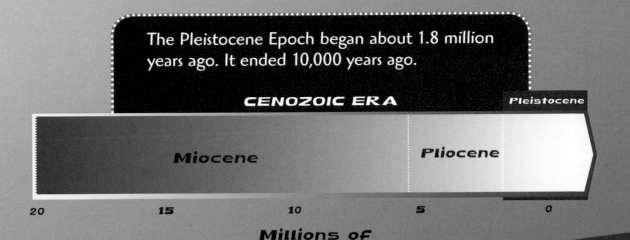

The Pleistocene Epoch began about 1.8 million years ago. It ended 10,000 years ago.

CENOZOIC ERA — Pleistocene

Miocene

Pliocene

20   15   10   5   0

Millions of Years Ago

In the *Ice Age* movies, Diego and Shira are both saber-toothed cats.

Smilodon lived during the Pleistocene Epoch. This is also called the Ice Age. During this time, large sheets of ice began to cover the earth. The saber-toothed cat lived south of the coldest icy glaciers. It roamed the forests and grasslands of what is now North America and South America.

SABER-TOOTHED CUBS

Little is known about the saber-toothed cat's life cycle. Females gave birth to live young. They may have had up to three cubs at one time.

Today's cats are born blind. They keep their eyes shut until they are two weeks old. It takes another week for them to see clearly. It is possible that saber-toothed cubs were also born this way.

Smilodon cubs were not born with large canine teeth. Like humans they likely had smaller teeth that later fell out. As the animal grew, its second set of longer, sharper teeth came in.

By the time they were 20 months old, saber-toothed cats were almost fully grown. This was the same time cubs began hunting for food with the pack.

THE FIRST FOSSILS

The first *Smilodon* fossils were discovered in 1841. Paleontologist Peter Wilhelm Lund found the cat's bones in caves near Lagoa Santa, Brazil. Since then thousands of *Smilodon* fossils have been found throughout North and South America.

One place holds more saber-toothed cat fossils than anywhere else. Bones from more than 2,000 *Smilodon* have been found in the La Brea tar pits in California. *Smilodon* likely tried to eat animals that had

gotten stuck in tar pits. Unfortunately the cats may have gotten stuck in the tar pits as well.

Smilodon is the official state fossil of California.

GOING EXTINCT

Although lions and other animals related to *Smilodon* are alive today, the prehistoric cat is extinct. Scientists have different ideas to explain why the animal may have died out. But no one is certain.

Some scientists believe that the animal died off because the climate changed. The saber-toothed cat may not have been able to survive the changing temperatures. It is also possible that weather changes made it difficult to find food. Others believe that early humans killed off the prehistoric cats.

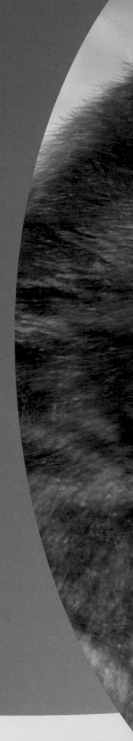

GLOSSARY

canine—one of the pointed teeth on each side of an animal's upper and lower jaws

climate—the average weather of a place throughout the year

epoch—an amount of time that is less than a geologic period and greater than a geologic age

extinct—no longer living; an extinct animal is one that has died out, with no more of its kind

glacier—a huge sheet of ice found in mountain valleys or polar regions; a glacier is formed when snow falls and does not melt because the temperature remains below freezing

mane—the long, thick hair on the head and neck of a male lion

mate—the male or female partner of a pair of animals

paleontologist—a scientist who studies fossils and other ancient life forms

Pleistocene—the epoch beginning two million years ago and ending 10,000 years ago

predator—an animal that hunts other animals for food

prehistoric—living or occurring before people began to write history

prey—an animal hunted by another animal for food

retractable—to draw or pull back

CRITICAL THINKING QUESTIONS

1. How were saber-toothed cats similar to today's lions? How were they different?

2. What is the most well known saber-toothed cat? Use the text to help you with your answer.

3. Saber-toothed cats lived during the Ice Age. Name two other types of animals alive during this time.

READ MORE

Gilbert, Sara. *Saber-toothed Cats*. Ice Age Mega Beasts. Mankato, Minn.: Creative Paperbacks, 2017.

Oachs, Emily Rose. *Timeline Science: The Ice Age*. Timeline Science. San Diego: Silver Dolphin Books, 2017.

Zieger, Jennifer. *Saber-Toothed Cat*. 21st Century Junior Library. Ann Arbor, Mich.: Cherry Lake Publishing, 2016.

INTERNET SITES

Use FactHound to find Internet sites related to this book.

Visit *www.facthound.com*

Just type in 9781543505382 and go.

Check out projects, games and lots more at
www.capstonekids.com

INDEX